Classic Farm Tractors

An Album of Favorite Farm Tractors from 1900–1970

By Cletus Hohman

Voyageur Press

Edited by Michael Dregni and Margret Aldrich
Series design by Andrea Rud
Printed in Hong Kong

01   02   03   04   05   5   4   3   2   1

Library of Congress Cataloging-in-Publication Data
Hohman, Cletus.
    Classic farm tractors : an album of favorite farm tractors from 1900–1970 / by Cletus Hohman.
        p. cm.
    ISBN 0-89658-566-2 (alk. paper)
    1. Farm tractors—History. 2. Antique and classic tractors. I. Title.

TL233.6.F37 H64 2001
631.3'72'0904—dc21

                    2001039019

1015

Distributed in Canada by Raincoast Books, 9050 Shaughnessy Street, Vancouver, B.C. V6P 6E5

Published by Voyageur Press, Inc.
123 North Second Street, P.O. Box 338, Stillwater, MN 55082 U.S.A.
651-430-2210, fax 651-430-2211
books@voyageurpress.com
www.voyageurpress.com

Educators, fundraisers, premium and gift buyers, publicists, and marketing managers: Looking for creative products and new sales ideas? Voyageur Press books are available at special discounts when purchased in quantities, and special editions can be created to your specifications. For details contact the marketing department at 800-888-9653.

On the frontispiece:
Thrills—and spills—abounded when Pa brought home the family's new Farmall.

On the title pages:
The Deere New Generation: A 1960 Model 3010 and 1960 Model 4010. Owner: Kenny Smith. (Photograph by Chester Peterson Jr.)

Inset on the title pages:
Only a Ford-Ferguson 9N was up to the task of hauling bumper sugar beet crops in this "tall-tale" collage postcard from the 1940s.

Legal Notice
This is not an official publication of Deere & Co., Caterpillar Inc., AGCO/Allis-Chalmers, CNH Global NV, or Fiat. Certain names, model designations, and logo designs are the property of trademark holders. We use them for identification purposes only. Neither the author, photographer, publisher, nor this book are in any way affiliated with Deere & Co., Caterpillar Inc., AGCO/Allis-Chalmers, CNH Global NV, or Fiat.

Contents

Threshing day
A 1920s threshing crew feeds a separator powered by a Minneapolis-Moline Twin City tractor.

Farewell Horses, Hello Tractors

The Dawn of a New Era in Farming

Above: **Proud Farmall owners**
Ma, Pa, and Spot pose proudly with the family's Farmall.

Facing page: **Horse farming**
A team of six workhorses pulls a plow through the prairie soil, kicking up a dust cloud that engulfs the driver. (Photograph by Hans Halberstadt)

In the beginning, crops were planted, tended, and harvested by hand. Wooden, and then steel, tools were crafted, and the earliest farmers were suddenly able to farm larger plots and raise more food. Horse and oxen teams were harnessed to pull plows, and again the amount of land one farmer could steward increased. From the dawn of agriculture to the mid 1800s, however, advances in farming were slow.

Along with the 1800s came a series of mechanical inventions that revolutionized agriculture as never before. Within a period of some forty years, Cyrus Hall McCormick's reaper of 1831, the refinement of the threshing machine in the 1860s, and John F. Appleby's amazing Appleby Automatic Knotter of 1875 all changed the face of farming forever. Yet these inventions still relied on animals for power, which was a grave limitation. Power was the key to the future.

The Industrial Age arrived on the farm in the 1880s in the form of steam engines that could power separators. With the development of drivetrains, the steam traction engine could pull a plow. And as internal-combustion engines replaced the steamers at the dawn of the 1900s, gas tractors slowly found a place on almost every farm in the nation. By the 1920s, many a farmer bade a sad farewell to Old Dobbin as the horse was traded in on a Farmall or a Johnny Popper.

It was the dawn of a new era in farming.

CHAPTER 1

The Age of Steam, 1860s–1910s

Building Up a Head of Steam

Steam power—the harnessed energy created by hot water vapors—revolutionized agriculture as few things had up until the mid 1800s. The first steam engines were merely powerplants on wheels and had to be pulled somewhat ignominiously into place by a team of horses or oxen. Once it was situated, the steam engine was hooked to a seperator via a long leather belt, making it ready to provide continuous power beyond anyone's imagination—so long as the firebox was fed, the water supply did not dry up, and the steam pressure did not get high enough to blow up the boiler.

Steam traction engines were developed from the first horse-drawn steam engines. In the hands of an able steam "engineer," these refined machines could power themselves through farm fields, pulling countless plow bottoms. With this mechanical horsepower, the vast expanses of prairie sod could be broken with ease.

Farmers could now raise more grain than they ever dreamed possible, selling the bounty to markets around the globe. And the companies such as J. I. Case, Advance-Rumely, Avery, Holt, Best, Gaar-Scott, and others who built the steam tractors also built their fortunes on steam power.

Above: **Threshing days**
An old-timer shows the new generation how the threshing operation works in this advertising painting from the J. I. Case Company of Racine, Wisconsin.

Facing page: **Advance steamer**
A steam tractor built by the Advance Thresher Company of Battle Creek, Michigan, waits patiently while a horse team finishes its work before taking to the field. Advance was purchased by the Rumely Company of La Porte, Indiana, and became the famous Advance-Rumely Thresher Company. (Photograph by Hans Halberstadt)

Threshing crew
An 1880s threshing crew halts work to pose for a photograph with its steam traction engine at the center of the action. (Fred Hultstrand History in Pictures Collection, NDIRS-NDSU, Fargo)

Illinois steamer

A mammoth steamer built by the Illinois Thresher Company of Sycamore, Illinois, pulls a hay wagon. Only farmers with huge farm operations could afford to purchase, use, and maintain large steamers such as this Illinois. Until affordable gasoline-engine tractors became available, family farmers had to hire custom threshing outfits. (Photograph by Hans Halberstadt)

11

Below: **Steamer controls**
"A good steam engineer should be sober, industrious, careful, and faithful to his charge," admonished the *Young Engineer's Guide,* a steam-engine instruction book published by J. I. Case in the early 1900s. Faced with this array of controls, levers, and gauges, it was advice that was well heeded. (Photograph by Hans Halberstadt)

Above: **Avery Undermounted**
The Avery Company of Peoria, Illinois, was famed for its Undermounted steamer engineered by John Bartholomew in 1909. The Undermounted was a locomotive-style steamer with two cylinders mounted beneath the boiler. Renowned for their smooth and quiet operation, Avery built 16-, 18-, 20-, 30-, 40-, and 50-hp Undermounteds. Owner: Jim Briden. (Photograph by Hans Halberstadt)

Busting the prairie

A steamer pulls a fourteen–bottom plow to cut through the virgin prairie. (Fred Hultstrand History in Pictures Collection, NDIRS-NDSU, Fargo)

Holt steamer

A steamer built by Benjamin Holt's Holt Manufacturing Company of Stockton, California, hauls two wagons laden with old-growth logs from a Pacific Northwest forest.

14

Above: **Stoking the firebox**

Dressed in his best engineer's overalls, a fireman stokes the Best steamer's firebox. (Photograph by Hans Halberstadt)

Left: **Best steamer**

The principal rival of Ben Holt was Daniel Best, whose Daniel Best Agricultural Works of San Leandro, California, built this giant in the 1890s and 1900s. In 1908, Holt bought Best's firm, laying the foundation for the Caterpillar Tractor Company. Owner: Oakland, California, Museum Ardenwood Historic Farm. (Photograph by Hans Halberstadt)

CHAPTER 2

Pioneering Farm Power, 1900s–1920s

From the Dominance of the Fordson to the Advent of the Farmall

Above: Farewell to Old Dobbin

In this 1910s brochure, J. I. Case explained how its Crossmotor tractor could replace twelve horses.

Facing page: Allis-Chalmers Model E 20/35

Built from 1923 to 1930, the Model E 20/35 was the flagship of the Allis-Chalmers Company of Milwaukee, Wisconsin. The tractor was powered by a four-cylinder vertical I-head, valve-in-head engine displacing 460.7 ci (7,546 cc). Owner: Steve Rosenboom. (Photograph by Chester Peterson Jr.)

Steam tractors were typically large, expensive machines affordable only to the operators of gigantic farms. The majority of family farmers could not afford steam power, except at threshing time when a custom threshing crew and its steam traction engine was often hired.

With the refinement of Nikolas Otto's four-cycle, internal-combustion engine, gasoline-fueled tractors were introduced. Soon garages, workshops, and fledgling factories were building gas tractors of numerous types, from oddball Rube Goldberg contraptions to truly innovative machines that took the burden of farming off the farmer and the horse's back and put it on mechanical horsepower.

It was with the 1917 introduction of Henry Ford's Fordson, however, that an inexpensive, lightweight gas tractor was finally available for most farms. By the mid 1920s, 80 percent of the farm tractors at work around the globe were Fordsons. It was not until 1924 when International Harvester introduced its refined Farmall that the Fordson's reign was challenged.

Above: **Ford doodlebug**

When only large steamers were available, many farmers converted their old Ford Model T automobiles into home-brewed mechanical mules. Fondly known as "doodlebugs," these Ford-powered tractors could be built from kits or plans supplied by numerous firms throughout North America in the 1900s and 1910s. (Photograph by Chester Peterson Jr.)

Right: **Ford tractor plans**

The Pullford Company of Quincy, Illinois, was just one of many enterprising firms to offer conversion kits to resurrect Ford Model T automobiles as farm tractors.

18

Above: **Common Sense V-8**

Pioneering tractors were offered by numerous fledgling firms during the 1900s and 1910s. The Common Sense gas tractor from the Minneapolis, Minnesota, company of the same name featured a stunning 20/40 V-8 engine. The tractor made its debut in 1915, but even the radical eight-cylinder powerplant could not win it fans, and the Common Sense was history by 1920.

Below: **Waterloo Boy Model N**

The Waterloo Gasoline Engine Company of Waterloo, Iowa, introduced its great Waterloo Boy in 1915. Powered by an overhead-valve, two-cylinder engine of 465 ci (7,617 cc), it made 25 belt hp. Deere & Company of Moline, Illinois, bought the Waterloo concern in 1918, and continued building the Model N until 1924. Deere's development of the Waterloo Boy, to be named the Model D, was released in 1923 painted with Deere's own logo. Owner: Doug Peltzer. (Photograph by Hans Halberstadt)

Above: Fordson Model F

Built from 1918 to 1928 as the Fordson Model F and from 1929 to 1946 as the Model N, Henry Ford's Fordson was a revolutionary lightweight and inexpensive tractor that brought power farming to the world. Weighing just 2,700 pounds (1,215 kg), the Fordson was powered by a 251-ci (4,111-cc) side-valve, four-cylinder engine. (Photograph by Hans Halberstadt)

Left, top: **Fordson brochure**

Left, bottom: **"Minneapolis" Ford**

The "Minneapolis" Ford is without doubt history's most infamous tractor. The Ford Tractor Company of Minneapolis, Minnesota, was started in 1914 with hopes that Henry Ford would buy rights to the name. Ford instead called his company Henry Ford & Son and named his machine the Fordson. The "Minneapolis" Ford later inspired disgruntled farmer Wilmot Crozier to run for election to the Nebraska legislature, where he penned the famous Nebraska Tractor Test Law of 1919.

Holt Model 75

Ben Holt's Model 75 was powered by a massive 1,400-ci (22,932-cc) four-cylinder engine that produced 50 drawbar and 75 belt hp. Watching one of Holt's pioneering treaded tractors at work in 1905, photographer Charles Clements remarked, "She crawls along like a caterpillar," and a name was born. Owner: Koster family. (Photograph by Hans Halberstadt)

Far left: Rumely OilPull 12/20 Type K

Advance-Rumely's OilPull Type K was built from 1919 to 1924. The prolific OilPull line used oil instead of water as a coolant. The line made its debut in 1910 with the 25/45 Type B and continued through 1930. Owner: Kent Kaster. (Photograph by Chester Peterson Jr.)

Left: **Rumely's *OilPull Magazine***

Renault

French tractor maker Renault of Billancourt, Paris, began building tractors in the 1910s, offering various crawlers, wheeled tractors, and four-wheel-drive machines. This patriotic Renault advertisement implored that "The French earth should be farmed by a French tractor." The Renault firm was nationalized in 1945 and still builds tractors today.

Moline Universal Model C

Produced by the Moline Plow Company of Moline, Illinois, from 1918 to 1923, the Universal set a style for early lightweight tractors that was licensed by numerous other makers. The Universal was powered by a 192-ci (3,145-cc) four-cylinder engine that created 27 belt hp. Owner: Walter Keller. (Photograph © Andrew Morland)

Above: Case Crossmotor
Case's revolutionary Crossmotors debuted in 1918 with a cast-iron unit frame that housed the engine crankshaft and transmission. A variety of models were offered until 1928 with power from the lightweight 9/18B to the monster 40/72. (Photograph by Hans Halberstadt)

Left: Case brochure
Case promised that its tractors brought "The Dawn of a Brighter Day" compared with horse farming.

Nilson

Tractor manufacturers proliferated in the 1910s and 1920s, but many were wiped out by the recession following World War I and the depression of the 1930s. The Nilson Tractor Company of Minneapolis, Minnesota, started operations in 1913 and offered a variety of three- and four-wheeled machines until the firm's demise at the dawn of the Great Depression in 1929. (Photograph by Hans Halberstadt)

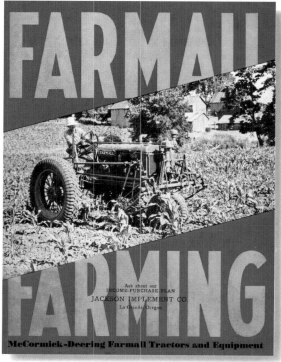

Above: **Farmall Farming brochure**

Left: **Farmall F-20**
The International Harvester Company of Chicago, Illinois, launched its radical Farmall general-purpose tractor in 1924. The machine was capable of "farming all," as its name implied: Not only could it handle draft and belt duties, it also boasted a rear power takeoff (PTO) for running harvesters and the crop clearance necessary for cultivating. The initial Farmall Regular would be followed by a long lineage of models, including this F-20 of 1932–1939. Owner: Ira Matheney. (Photograph by Hans Halberstadt)

Deere Model D

Deere was a latecomer to the tractor field, but when its Model D debuted in 1923, the company's reputation as a serious tractor maker was cemented. The D became an industry standard and remained in production until 1953. It was Deere's development of the Waterloo Boy, which Deere purchased rights to in 1918. The first D's featured 465-ci (7,617-cc) engines; displacement was increased to 501 ci (8,206 cc) in 1927. By the end of the line, the D produced 42 belt hp from its overhead-valve four-cylinder. (Photographs by Hans Halberstadt)

Right: **Lanz Bulldog HL 12 hp**

Heinrich Lanz of Mannheim, Germany, began building tractors in 1911 but became famous the world over for its Bulldog model engineered by Dr. Fritz Huber and launched in 1921. The Bulldog was the world's first hot-bulb-fired, crude-oil-burning tractor, and would be licensed by tractor makers around the globe as well as inspire many imitators. Owner: John Deere–Lanz Museum. (Photograph © Andrew Morland)

Below: **Lanz Bulldog brochure**

Deere Model GPO

Deere's answer to the general-purpose Farmall arrived in 1928 as the Model C, soon renamed the Model GP. In the end, the GP was only a transitional model before the debut of the Models A and B in 1935, but it became famous during its brief production period anyway. The GPO orchard version was built in only 1931–1935 and boasted a wide front end. Owner: Doug Peltzer. (Photograph by Hans Halberstadt)

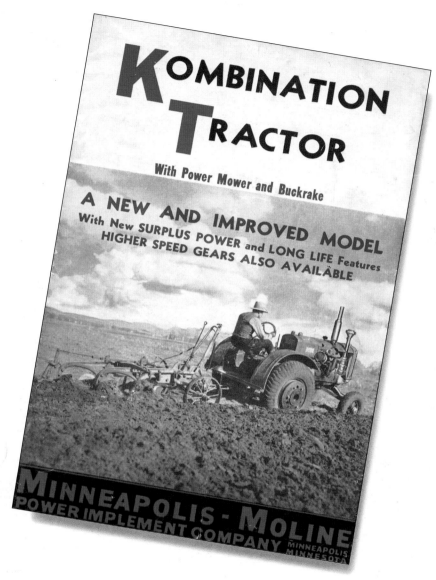

Above: **Minneapolis-Moline Kombination Tractor brochure**

Right: **Minneapolis-Moline Twin City Kombination Tractor**
The Twin City KT was developed by the Minneapolis Steel & Machinery Company of Minneapolis, Minnesota, and remained in the tractor lineup after MS&M merged with two other firms in 1929 to form the Minneapolis-Moline Company of Minneapolis. The KT was an attempt to modify a standard tractor to do row-crop work. Owner: Curtis Rink. (Photograph by Chester Peterson Jr.)

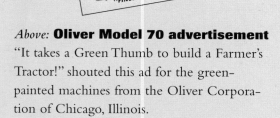

Above: **Oliver Model 70 advertisement**

"It takes a Green Thumb to build a Farmer's Tractor!" shouted this ad for the green-painted machines from the Oliver Corporation of Chicago, Illinois.

Facing page: **Massey-Harris General Purpose 15/22**

The old and the new: A 1936 Massey-Harris GP 15/22 stands in the foreground while a horse team finishes its work. The Massey-Harris Company of Toronto, Ontario, had roots back to 1891 but did not offer a tractor until 1917. The four-wheel-drive General Purpose of 1930–1936 was a revolutionary machine—perhaps too revolutionary, as it remained in production only six years. The GP predated the large articulated four-wheel drives of the 1960s by some three decades. Owner: Glen Doring. (Photograph by Hans Halberstadt)

CHAPTER 3

Transforming Agriculture, 1930s–1940s

Johnny Poppers, Comfortractors, Bulldogs, and a Tractor for Every Farm

The revolution brought on by the gas tractor transformed farming. By the mid 1920s, gas tractors were inexpensive enough that almost every farmer could afford one and refined enough that it didn't take a wizard with a wrench and a large vocabulary of curses to operate it. "Power farming" was here to stay.

Along the way, the tractor also played a hand in transforming the social fabric of farming. A farmer with a tractor was now more self-sufficient and independent, not needing a large crew of hired hands or friendly neighbors to share in the harvest or threshing chores. Something was lost in the farm community, and as the gas tractor began to separate the farmer from his neighbor, it also played a hand in speeding the long emigration of people from the farm to the city.

The farm-equipment-manufacturing industry was also transformed through these decades. While there were more than two hundred different farm tractor companies hawking their wares in the 1910s, the recession following World War I and the dawn of the Great Depression of the 1930s whittled down the number of companies until just several dozen remained. Many tractors were orphaned by bankruptcy, mergers, and takeovers, and lost to history.

Allis-Chalmers Model U

Built originally as the United Tractor for the United Tractor and Equipment Distributors' Association of Chicago, Illinois, starting in 1929, the machine was also sold by Allis as the Model U. Allis's U became the first tractor mounted on pneumatic rubber tires as a standard feature. Pneumatic tires signaled a revolution in farming—not to mention a revolution in comfort for farmers! Owners: Edwin and Larry Karg. (Photograph by Chester Peterson Jr.)

Cletrac Model 15

Rollin White's Cleveland Tractor Company of Cleveland, Ohio, built the Cletrac crawlers that competed with Caterpillar. Debuting in 1930, the diminutive Model 15 boast 15 hp, making it ideal for light-duty chores and orchard work. It was powered by a Hercules four-cylinder engine. Owner: Bill Bechtold. (Photograph by Hans Halberstadt)

All photos: Deere Model BW

Deere's "Johnny Popper" lineage included the famous Model B, introduced in 1935 and produced until 1960 as the updated Model 530. This unstyled BW featured a two-cylinder, 149-ci (2,441-cc) engine and the wide front end, denoted by the "W" suffix. Standard-tread BR, single-front-wheel BN, industrial BI, orchard BO wheeled and crawler versions, and Hi-Crop BNH and BWH models were all offered. By the 530, the tractor had 39 belt hp available. (Photographs by Hans Halberstadt)

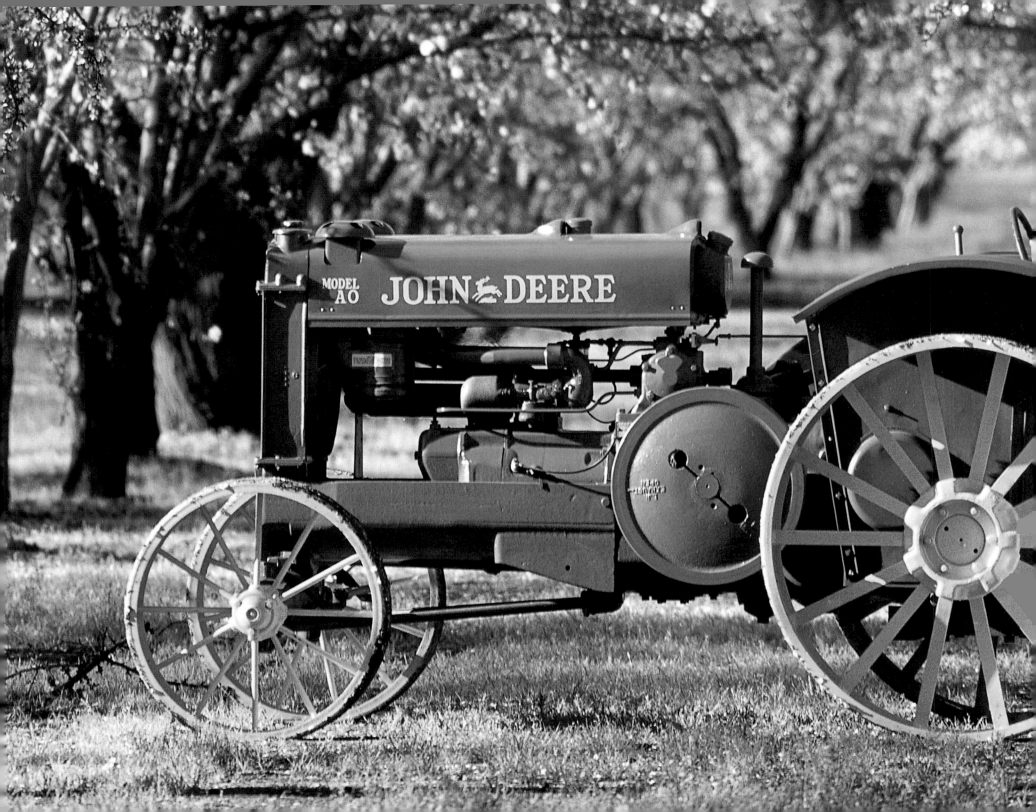

Deere Model AO

The larger sibling to the Model B, Deere's Model A line was launched a year earlier than the B, in 1934. Like the B, the A was available in many variations, including the AR, AO, AOS streamlined, AN, AW, ANH, AWH, and AI. The legacy of the A continued through the 630 of 1958–1960. Owner: Irv Baker. (Photographs by Hans Halberstadt)

Facing page: **Deere Model BO**
The orchard Model BO was dressed up with full fenders, a wide front, cowling over hood-top fixtures, and a low exhaust pipe so the tractor did not pose a danger to orchard trees. Owner: Doug Peltzer. (Photograph by Hans Halberstadt)

Above and left: **Allis-Chalmers Model WC**
Introduced in 1933, the WC was Allis-Chalmers's row-crop machine whereas the WF of 1940 was the standard-tread version. With a four-cylinder, 201-ci (3,292-cc) engine, it produced 14.36 drawbar and 21.48 belt hp. The WC was the first tractor to feature a "square" engine where the bore and stroke were equal. The WD replaced the WC in 1948 and continued as the WD-45 until 1957. Owner: Steve Rosenboom. (Photographs by Chester Peterson Jr.)

All photos: **McCormick-Deering 10/20 Orchard**

International Harvester's 10/20 was launched in 1923 as a smaller sibling to the epochal 15/30 of 1921. Its four-cylinder, 284-ci (4,652-cc) engine cranked out 20 belt hp. This 1924 Orchard variation featured the usual full fenders and a low, protected muffler. Owner: Doug Peltzer. (Photographs by Hans Halberstadt)

McCormick-Deering O-12

With the debut of the Farmall, International soon offered purpose-built variations on the regular, row-crop model, including this Orchard version of the smaller F-12. The O-12 of 1935–1938 was a compact, lightweight, and inexpensive machine for the small orchard grower. Owner: Dan Schmidt. (Photograph by Hans Halberstadt)

Both photos: Case Model RC

Launched in 1935, the RC was Case's row-crop challenger to the Farmall and Deere's Model B. With its side-valve, four-cylinder Waukesha engine, the RC was in the same power class as the Farmall F-12. The R Series was superseded by the S and SC models in 1941. Owner: Dale Hartley. (Photographs by Hans Halberstadt)

Far left and left: **Minneapolis-Moline Model UDLX**

Minneapolis-Moline's flagship tractor was known by a variety of names: the U-Deluxe, UDLX, and the Comfortractor. When it made its debut in 1938, it was the Cadillac of farm tractors, boasting a top speed of 40 mph (64 km/h), five-speed transmission, enclosed cab, windshield wipers, crank-out windows, heater, speedometer, cigar lighter, high- and low-beam headlamps, and seating for three. It was designed as a tractor that could plow all week and then be driven to town on Saturday. Sadly, it was too much too soon, and production lasted only until 1941. Owner: Roger Mohr. (Photographs by Chester Peterson Jr.)

Minneapolis-Moline neon dealer sign

Ford-Ferguson 9N

Henry Ford revolutionized farming with his Fordson of 1918—and did it again in 1939 with his 9N. This time the Ford Motor Company of Dearborn, Michigan, had the help of brilliant but eccentric Irishman Harry Ferguson, who created the tractor's three-point draft-control hitch. Debuting in 1939, the 9N was superseded by the stripped-down wartime 2N of 1942–1947. This was one of the first 9Ns, denoted by its horizontal-louvered grill. Owner: Dwight Emstrom. (Photograph by Chester Peterson Jr.)

FLEXIBLE FARMING
FASTER · EASIER · MORE PROFITABLE

Rejuvenating a pasture

Above: **Ford-Ferguson 2N**

Ever patriotic, Henry Ford introduced in 1942 the 2N, which saved on war-critical materials. The 2N eschewed rubber to ride on steel wheels and had neither a starter nor generator to save on copper. After World War II, 2Ns boasted the full complement of equipment like their 9N predecessors. Owner: Palmer Fossum. (Photograph by Chester Peterson Jr.)

Ford-Ferguson 9N brochure

Lanz HR9 Eil Bulldog

Introduced in 1937, Lanz's "Speedy" Bulldog was similar in concept to Minneapolis-Moline's UDLX. The Eil Bulldog boasted a comfortable driving environment protected by a full windshield; open- and closed-cab versions were available. With power from a 629-ci (10,303-cc) engine and 55 hp on tap, these Bulldog road models had five or six forward gears and a top speed of 25 mph (40 km/h). Owner: Pierre Bouillé. (Photograph © Andrew Morland)

Below: **Oliver Model 70 brochure**

When it was launched in 1935, the Oliver 70 was a giant step forward in tractor technology. It boasted a six-cylinder engine with an electric starter and was one of the first tractors designed to run on the new 70-octane gasoline, hence the designation "70." In 1937, the Fleetline Series redesign dressed the 70 in stylish new sheet metal.

THE STURDY "70" ROW CROP

70

IT'S BETTER TO BUY AN OLIVER—THAN TO WISH YOU HAD

OLIVER

Above: **Silver King R-38**

Made by a railroad locomotive constructor, the Fate-Root-Heath Company of Plymouth, Ohio, the Silver King was originally known as the Plymouth tractor. The standard-tread R-38 of 1933–1939 was accompanied by the row-crop R-66 of 1936–1939. Power came from a side-valve, 133-ci (2,178-cc) four-cylinder capable of 20 hp. Silver King production ended in 1956. Owner: Dilbert Fidler. (Photograph by Hans Halberstadt)

Above: **Graham-Bradley advertisement**

In 1938, the Graham-Paige Motors Corporation of Chicago, Illinois, launched its 503.103 tricycle tractor for sale through the grand mail-order firm of Sears, Roebuck & Company of Chicago. The tractor was called the Graham-Bradley as the Bradley name had been used by Sears for farm items for years. A wide-front 503.104 was offered from 1939 to 1941. Both machines were powered by a 218-ci (3,571-cc), side-valve six-cylinder that produced 30 PTO hp.

Right: **Case Model RC**

Styling came to farm tractors in the 1930s with streamlining and ergonomics recasting tractors as being easier to operate and service. Case updated its R Series with a new cast grill, rounded hoodline, and brilliant Flambeau Red paint. (Photograph by Hans Halberstadt)

Facing page: **Schlüter DZM25**

Motorenfabrik Anton Schlüter of Munich, Germany, began building tractors in 1937. This early, 1939 DZM25 was powered by a two-cylinder, 165-ci (2,703-cc) diesel that produced 25 hp. Owner: Nick Baldwin. (Photograph © Andrew Morland)

Above: **Allis-Chalmers Model B brochure**

Facing page: **Ford 8N High-Crop**
When Henry Ford died, the Handshake Agreement between Ford and Harry Ferguson died as well. The Ford Motor Company usurped many of Ferguson's patented design concepts when it launched its 8N of 1947–1952. Ferguson retaliated with a massive lawsuit that took many years to settle, and then built his own version of the Ford 9N as the Ferguson TE-20. Both the 8N and TE-20 were great tractors; they should have been, as they came from nearly identical blueprints. Owner: Dwight Emstrom. (Photograph by Chester Peterson Jr.)

CHAPTER 4

The Golden Years of the Farm Tractor, 1950s–1960s

Tractors of Every Color, from Prairie Gold to Flambeau Red to Poppin' Johnny Green

The years following World War II were the best of times and the worst of times for the farm tractor. Tractors were now viewed as an essential part of the farm, and more tractors were being built than ever before. Mechanical refinements such as power takeoffs, hydraulic systems, articulation, four-wheel drive, diesel engines, multi-ratio transmissions, and ergonomics continued to create better machines.

Yet trouble lay ahead. In the mid 1950s, farm-equipment manufacturers were glutted with tractors, and the industry experienced another of its periodic turnovers. At the dawn of the gas tractor's rise in the 1910s, there had been more than two hundred different makes of tractors available. After the recession following World War I and the turmoil of the Great Depression, the industry was reduced to several dozen manufacturers. By the year 2000, the industry was ruled by less than six major makers around the globe.

In the process, the farm tractor came full circle. As in the olden days of the mammoth steam traction engines, tractors became gigantic and expensive machines once again, built to farm huge tracts of land for large farm operations.

These dramatic changes in farm society fueled a nostalgia for the way things were. People began collecting tractors as well as almost anything and everything associated with the good old days down on the farm. They sought out old machines junked in windbreaks or stored away in barns, restored them to better-than-new condition, and proudly paraded them in fairs or hooked them up to run old separators at threshing-day revivals. The farm tractor had become recognized as a cultural icon of the farm.

Far left: **Deere Model HWH**
Styling came to Deere's green machines via renowned industrial stylist Henry Dreyfuss, who gave the "unstyled" Poppin' Johnnies a modern facelift in the late 1930s. The Model H debuted in 1939 with styled bodywork. This Hi-Crop, wide-front row-crop tractor was a rarity that was built only in 1941–1942. Owner: Doug Peltzer. (Photograph by Hans Halberstadt)

Left, top: **Ford-Ferguson 8N**
The 8N's controls were simplicity personified. (Photograph by Hans Halberstadt)

Left, bottom: **Cockshutt 30**
In 1946, the Cockshutt Plow Company of Brantford, Ontario, released the first tractor of its own design, the 30. It was the first production tractor to have a live PTO and was powered by a 30-hp, 153-ci (2,506-cc), four-cylinder Buda engine. (Photograph © Andrew Morland)

Above: **Minneapolis-Moline Model R**

The R was Minne-Mo's smallest tractor during its 1939–1954 production life with a 165-ci (2,703-cc), 26-hp four-cylinder. Like the UDLX, it could be equipped with a stylish enclosed cab, but lacked the Comfortractor's luxurious amenities. Owner: Roger Mohr. (Photograph by Chester Peterson Jr.)

Right: **Minneapolis-Moline calendar painting**

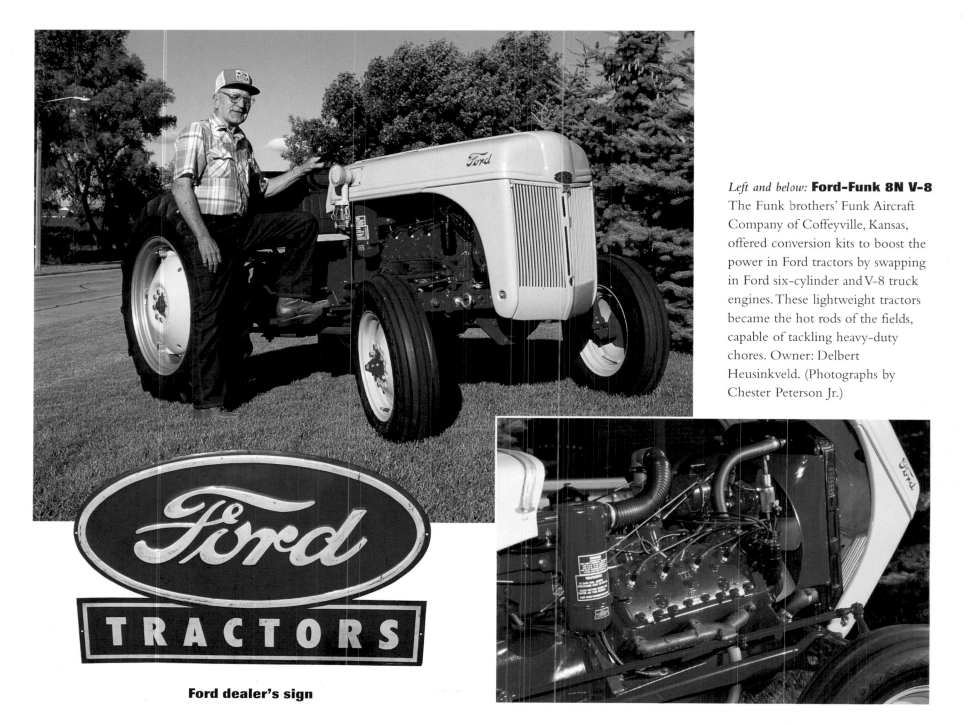

Left and below: **Ford-Funk 8N V-8**
The Funk brothers' Funk Aircraft Company of Coffeyville, Kansas, offered conversion kits to boost the power in Ford tractors by swapping in Ford six-cylinder and V-8 truck engines. These lightweight tractors became the hot rods of the fields, capable of tackling heavy-duty chores. Owner: Delbert Heusinkveld. (Photographs by Chester Peterson Jr.)

Ford dealer's sign

Oliver 70 Orchard

Dressed in fully enclosed bodywork, Oliver's 70 was ready for work in orchards and groves. The 70's 200-ci (3,276-cc) six-cylinder boasted a six-speed transmission. The Fleetline 70 of 1937–1948 was replaced by the 77 of 1947–1954. Owner: Everett Jensen. (Photographs by Hans Halberstadt)

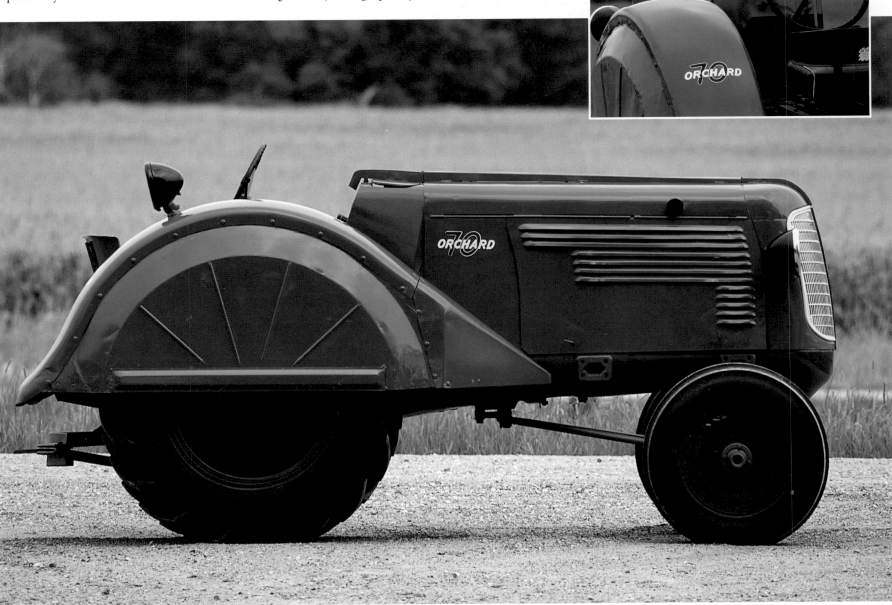

Left: **Allis-Chalmers Model B**

To battle the Farmall F-12, Allis-Chalmers unveiled its Model B in 1938 and created a long-lived classic that stayed in production until 1958. Even with its elfin 116-ci (1,900-cc) four-cylinder and just 16 belt hp, the B was capable of taking on big chores. Owner: Steve Rosenboom. (Photograph by Chester Peterson Jr.)

Below: **SAME tractors on show**

SAME (Società Anònima Motori Endothermic) of Italy began offering tractors in 1942, but built its most famous models following World War II. The SAME line was distributed worldwide: Here, the full lineup was on show at the Minnesota State Fair in the 1960s.

Massey-Harris brochure

Above and facing page: **Massey-Harris 44 Orchard**
In 1946, Massey-Harris unveiled its first postwar tractor, the 44, which was soon available in standard, row-crop, and orchard versions; a diesel was added in 1948. All versions used a 260-ci (4,259-cc) four-cylinder. The 44 won a reputation as a dependable farm machine. Owners: Betty and Dick Lamb. (Photographs by Hans Halberstadt)

Allis-Chalmers Model G
The uniquely configured G was basically a hoe on wheels for truck gardeners. Built from 1948 to 1955, the G was powered by a rear-mounted, 62-ci (1,016-cc) four-cylinder Continental engine that was similar to that used in the Farmall Cub. Owner: Steve Rosenboom. (Photograph by Chester Peterson Jr.)

Left: Minneapolis–Moline Model U
The venerable U Series debuted in 1938 as the UT, was renamed as the U in 1949, and continued on as the 1954 UB; production ended in 1957. The series included standard, row-crop, and high-clearance sugar-cane models as well as kerosene-, gasoline-, and LPG-fueled versions. Owner: Roger Mohr. (Photograph by Chester Peterson Jr.)

Facing page: Oliver Model 66 Wide-Front
Oliver's classy Fleetline Series included the Model 66. Gas, diesel, and LPG engines of 129 ci (2,113 cc) were offered, as well as a 144-ci (2,359-cc), distillate-burning engine. All were four-cylinders and produced around 20 hp. (Photograph © Andrew Morland)

Case Model LA

Case's 1940–1953 LA was part of a long series of tractors starting with the 1928 L and continuing to the 900 of 1957–1959. Whereas the L was painted in gray, the LA wore Case's new trademark Flambeau Red paint. It also boasted an optional electrical system and LPG engine. The diesel LAD debuted in 1952. Owner: John S. Black. (Photographs by Hans Halberstadt)

Allis-Chalmers Model CA

The CA was ideal for working around the farmyard. Its 125-ci (2,048-cc) four-cylinder featured 22.97 drawbar and 25.96 belt hp. Standard equipment included power-adjust rear wheels, live PTO, draft control, hydraulics, and Snap Coupler for mounted attachments. Owner: Donald Fanetti. (Photograph by Chester Peterson Jr.)

Porsche Super

Ferdinand Porsche was the Henry Ford of Germany. Designer of the Volkswagen (and Porsche cars), he also designed a *Volksschlepper*, or "People's Tractor," in 1937. Porsche began building the tractor in 1945. Production was taken over by Allgaier from 1949 to 1957, after which the Mannesmann group constructed Porsche tractors.

Above: Minneapolis-Moline Model Z

Unveiled in 1937, the Z was the first "Visionlined" Minne-Mo and wore the firm's fancy new Prairie Gold paint scheme with red trim. The smooth Visionlined styling aided the operator in viewing fieldwork. Owner: Roger Mohr. (Photograph by Chester Peterson Jr.)

Minneapolis-Moline Model Z "Visionlined" brochure

Above: **Landini L55**

Officine Landini Fabbrico of Reggio Emilia, Italy, entered the tractor market in 1925 with a 25/30 hot-bulb "Testa Calda" machine similar to the Lanz Bulldog. Landini continued to build hot-bulb tractors with huge single-cylinder engines through the 1950s; the flagship 55/60 L55 was launched in 1955 and continued Landini's tradition. Landini became part of Massey-Ferguson in 1960. (Photograph by Eric Dregni)

Left: **Landini advertising poster**

Left, top: Caterpillar D2 Orchard
Caterpillar pioneered diesel development for tractors, offering its first diesel machine in 1931. The D2 arrived in 1938 as the diesel sibling of the gas-fueled R2 and remained in the Cat line until 1960. This orchard tractor sported grill cowling. Owner: Bill Garnett. (Photograph by Hans Halberstadt)

Left, bottom: Ford Jubilee NAA
The 1953 NAA was the first all-new Ford tractor in the fourteen years since the 9N. It boasted an all-new hydraulic system and a new, overhead-valve engine. Owner: the Sparks family. This NAA had just been remanufactured by N-Complete of Wilkinson, Indiana. N-Complete owner Tom Armstrong is at the controls. (Photograph © Andrew Morland)

Facing page: Deere Model 60
The admired Model A was updated as the 60 in 1952 and continued as the flagship general-purpose Johnny Popper until 1956, when it was followed by the 620 and 630. The 60 boasted a power increase over the A, live hydraulics, and a PTO. Along with gasoline and distillate, an LPG-fueled version was also available. Owner: Doug Peltzer. (Photograph by Hans Halberstadt)

Farmall Super M

Industrial designer Raymond Loewy updated the venerable Farmall F-30 with stylish streamlining as the M of 1939. The model featured a new, 248-ci (4,062-cc), overhead-valve four-cylinder and other advances. It was joined by the 1941 MD diesel, the 1952 Super M and Super MD, an LPG version, and the 1954 M-TA with Torque Amplifier giving ten forward speeds. This flagship Farmall continued until 1958 as the 450. Owner: Robbie Soults. (Photographs by Hans Halberstadt)

Right: **Farmall AV**

The 1947–1958 Farmall Cub and 1939–1953 Farmall A featured the same configuration, but the A was the larger sibling to the diminutive Cub. The offset setup made both machines ideal for truck gardeners, and both could be had with a large catalog of implements. The AV was a special high-crop version of the standard model. (Photograph by Hans Halberstadt)

Below: **Minneapolis-Moline Model UB**

Minne-Mo's venerable U Series was upgraded in 1954 with the UB models featuring high-compression cylinder heads and more power. This LPG-fueled Special posted 50 hp. Owner: Roger Mohr. (Photograph by Chester Peterson Jr.)

Above: **Allis Chalmers Model WD-45**

Allis-Chalmers's mainstay workhorse in the 1950s was its WD-45, whose lineage could be traced back to the 1933–1948 WC. Power came from an overhead-valve, 226-ci (3,702-cc) four-cylinder, cranking out 39 belt hp. Introduced in 1953, the WD-45 remained in production until 1957. The diesel WD-45D was built from 1955 to 1957. Owners: Edwin and Larry Karg. (Photograph by Chester Peterson Jr.)

Left: **Fiat Diesel**

Fiat of Turin, Italy, was Europe's largest producer of tractors following World War II. The firm began building tractors in 1918 with its Modello 702. This compact Fiat diesel was on show accompanied by two admiring fans.

Below: **Massey-Ferguson 35**

After Harry Ferguson joined forces with Massey-Harris in 1953, the tried-and-true Ferguson TO-35 was recast as the Massey-Ferguson 35 of 1955–1957. The engine was a 134-ci (2,195-cc) Continental, although a 152-ci (2,490-cc), three-cylinder Perkins diesel was soon an option. Owner: McGinn Sales. (Photograph by Chester Peterson Jr.)

Above: **Farmall M V-8 Special**

The quest for more power inspired some farmers to build custom tractors by fitting truck or automobile engines into tractor chassis. This Farmall M was custom-built by Norm Sevick and his son Jeremy and powered by an International truck V-8. (Photograph © Andrew Morland)

Above: Lanz B Bulldog D2806

Lanz soldiered on into the 1950s with its famed hot-bulb Bulldogs. This 1954 D2806 was powered by a 226-ci (3,702-cc) one-cylinder that produced 28 hp. In 1955, Lanz was bought by Deere and started producing multi-cylinder machines. Owner: Daniel Binet. (Photograph © Andrew Morland)

Lanz Bulldog brochure

Below: **MAN 2R2**

Maschinenfabrik Augsburg-Nürnberg (MAN) of Germany launched its first tractor in 1924 with a four-cylinder diesel engine and built several series of farm machines through the next decades. In 1958, MAN constructed Porsche tractors and also built this 1958 45-hp 2R2. Owner: Christian Denis. (Photograph © Andrew Morland)

Above: **Oliver Model 99 Diesel**

Oliver's Model 99 boasted a long and prolific production life. Introduced in 1932, its revised 995 sibling was built until 1961. The 99 Diesel featured a six-cylinder engine whereas the Super 99 GM of 1957–1958 was powered by a two-cycle General Motors three-cylinder topped by a supercharger. (Photograph by Hans Halberstadt)

Above: **Hanomag R228**

The Hannoversche Maschinenbau of Germany built motor plows from 1912 and added crawler and wheeled tractors in 1919. This 1959 R228 was powered by a 24-hp, two-stroke engine. Owner: Hank Van Doorn. (Photograph © Andrew Morland)

Right: **Fendt Dieselross brochure**

Fendt of Marktoberdorf, Germany, offered its multi-purpose Dieselross tractors with Deutz diesel engines for more then four decades. In 1997, Fendt was acquired by AGCO of the United States.

Facing page: **Minneapolis-Moline 445**

Still painted in Prairie Gold garb, Minneapolis-Moline's new Number Series tractors offered numerous refinements and updates. This 1957 445 launched M-M's Ampli-Torc transmission, increasing gears from the standard five forward and one reverse to ten forward and two reverse. Owner: Roger Mohr. (Photograph by Chester Peterson Jr.)

Right, top: **Deutz D25S**

Deutz of Germany offered its first tractor in 1926 as the 14-hp MTH 222. This 1963 D25S was powered by a 104-ci (1,704-cc) two-cylinder. Owner: Jan Nijssen. (Photograph © Andrew Morland)

Right, bottom: **Ford 601 Workmaster**

Starting in 1955, Ford broke away from its tradition of offering just one tractor model and unveiled a whole line. The 600 Series of 1955–1957 was followed by the 1958–1961 601 Series. Owner: Kuckenbecker Tractor Company. (Photograph by Hans Halberstadt)

Above: **Massey-Ferguson 85 advertising postcard**

Left: **Massey-Ferguson 95 Super**
Massey-Ferguson's 95 Super was actually a Minneapolis-Moline G that was painted in M-F colors and sold by Massey dealers. Owners: Dan and Ken Peterman. (Photograph by Chester Peterson Jr.)

International Farmall 806

International kept its Farmall line alive for decades. The 1963–1967 Farmall 806 was IHC's competitor to Deere's landmark 4020. The 806 was the world's most powerful all-purpose tractor with 94.93 PTO hp. Power came from a 361-ci (5,913-cc) six-cylinder diesel version or a 301-ci (4,930-cc) gas or LPG engine. Owner: Jerry Mez. (Photograph by Chester Peterson Jr.)

Case 830 HC Comfort King

Flanked by a 1964 Case 130 garden tractor, this 1964 830 High Crop Comfort King row-crop stands tall. Backed by a Case-O-Matic transmission, the 830 was a powerful, 60-hp machine. Owners: Jay and J. R. Gyger. (Photograph by Chester Peterson Jr.)

Oliver 1610

Oliver became part of White Motor Corporation of Cleveland, Ohio, in 1960. The 1610 followed on the heels of the 1600 of 1962–1964 and was equipped with Oliver's tried-and-true six-cylinder engine. Owner: Duane Peterson. (Photograph by Chester Peterson Jr.)

88

Allis-Chalmers D12 Series II HC

Allis-Chalmers's 1959–1968 D10 and 1959–1967 D12 were variations of the same tractor. The D10 was designed for one-row cultivation and had a narrow tread, whereas the D12 had a wider front axle and two-row treads. This 1964 D12 featured a 149-ci (2,441-cc) engine with 29.43 drawbar and 33.32 belt hp. Owners: Edwin and Larry Karg. (Photograph by Chester Peterson Jr.)

89

Left, top: **Oliver 2150**

Oliver's workhorse in the late 1960s was its powerful Model 2150. Owners: Roger and Gene Uhlenhake. (Photograph by Chester Peterson Jr.)

Left, bottom: **International Farmall 1206**

The power race was on when IHC unveiled its 1206 in 1965. This 1966 1206 Turbo Diesel boasted 100 PTO hp from its 361-ci (5,913-cc) six-cylinder, backed by a sixteen-speed transmission. Owner: Jerry Mez. (Photograph by Chester Peterson Jr.)

Facing page: **Deere 4020 Diesel**

Due to its innovative hydraulic system, Deere's New Generation 4020 was one of the most significant tractors of all time, and thus one of the most copied. The 1963–1972 4020 was offered in row-crop, high-crop, and standard versions with 88-hp gas, 90-hp LPG, and 91-hp diesel engines. (Photograph by Chester Peterson Jr.)

Bibliography

Baldwin, Nick and Andrew Morland. *Classic Tractors of the World: A-to-Z Coverage of the World's Most Fascinating Tractors*. Stillwater, Minnesota: Voyageur Press, 1998.

Grooms, Lynn K., Chester Peterson Jr., and Bill Huxley. *Vintage Allis-Chalmers Tractors: The Ultimate Tribute to Allis-Chalmers Tractors*. Stillwater, Minnesota: Voyageur Press, 2000.

Letourneau, Peter. *Vintage Case Tractors*. Stillwater, Minnesota: Voyageur Press, 1997.

Macmillan, Don. *The Big Book of John Deere Tractors: The Complete Model-by-Model Encyclopedia . . . Plus Brochures and Collectibles*. Stillwater, Minnesota: Voyageur Press, 1999.

Pripps, Robert N. and Andrew Morland. *The Big Book of Caterpillar: The Complete History of Caterpillar Bulldozers & Tractors . . . Plus Collectibles, Sales Memorabilia, and Brochures*. Stillwater, Minnesota: Voyageur Press, 2000.

Pripps, Robert N. and Andrew Morland. *The Big Book of Farm Tractors: The Complete History of the American Tractor 1855 to Present . . . Plus Brochures and Collectibles*. Stillwater, Minnesota: Voyageur Press, 2001.

Pripps, Robert N. and Andrew Morland. *The Big Book of Massey Tractors: The Complete History of Massey-Harris and Massey-Ferguson Tractors . . . Plus Collectibles, Sales Memorabilia, and Brochures*. Stillwater, Minnesota: Voyageur Press, 2001.

Pripps, Robert N. and Andrew Morland. *The Field Guide to Vintage Farm Tractors*. Stillwater, Minnesota: Voyageur Press, 1999.

Pripps, Robert N. and Andrew Morland. *Vintage Ford Tractors: The Ultimate Tribute to Ford, Fordson, Ferguson, and New Holland Tractors*. Stillwater, Minnesota: Voyageur Press, 1997.

Sanders, Ralph W. *Vintage Farm Tractors: The Ultimate Tribute to Classic Tractors*. Stillwater, Minnesota: Voyageur Press, 1996.

Sanders, Ralph W. *Vintage International Harvester Tractors: The Ultimate Tribute to International Harvester, Farmall, and McCormick-Deering Tractors*. Stillwater, Minnesota: Voyageur Press, 1997.

Tractor Clubs and Magazines

Advance Rumely
Rumely Collectors News
Scott Thompson
12109 Mennonite Church Road
Tremont, IL 61568

Allis-Chalmers
Old Allis News
Nan Jones
10925 Love Road
Bellevue, MI 49021–9250

The Allis Connection
Cheryl Deppe
8480 225th Avenue
Maquoketa, IA 52060

Upper Midwest A–C Club
22241 200th Street
Hutchinson, MN 55350

J. I. Case
J. I. Case Collectors Association
Old Abe's News
Dave Erb
400 Carriage Drive
Plain City, OH 43064

Caterpillar
Antique Caterpillar Machinery Owners Club
10816 Monitor-McKee Road NE
Woodburn, OR 97071

Cockshutt

International Cockshutt Club
Cockshutt Quarterly
Nick Jonknan
Route 2
Wyoming, Ontario N0N 1T0 Canada

Ferguson

The Ferguson Club and Journal
Sutton House
Sutton, Tenbury Wells
Worcestershire WR15 8RJ
Great Britain

Ford

9N–2N–8N–NAA Newsletter
Gerard and Bob Rinaldi
PO Box 275
East Corinth, VT 05040–0275

Ford/Fordson Collectors Association
645 Loveland-Miamiville Road
Loveland, OH 45140

International Harvester

IH Collectors Association
310 Busse Highway, Suite 250
Park Ridge, IL 60068–3251

Red Power
Daryl Miller
Box 277
Battle Creek, IA 51006

John Deere

Green Magazine
Richard Hain
2652 Davey Road
Bee, NE 68314–9132

Two-Cylinder Magazine
PO Box 10
Grundy Center, IA 50638–0010

Massey-Harris-Ferguson

Massey Collectors Association
Dale Lawrence
13607 Missouri Bottom Road
Bridgeton, MO 63044

Massey Collector's News
Wild Harvest
Keith Oltrogge
Box 529
Denver, IA 50622

Minneapolis-Moline

The Minneapolis-Moline Collectors Club
Dan Shima
409 Sheridan Drive
Eldridge, IA 52748

M-M Corresponder
Roger Mohr
3693 M Avenue
Vail, IA 51465

The Prairie Gold Rush
Ken Delap
17390 South SR 58
Seymour, IN 47274

Oliver–Hart-Parr

The Hart-Parr/Oliver Collector Association
The Hart-Parr/Oliver Collector
P.O. Box 685
Charles City, IA 50616

General Tractor Magazines

Antique Power
Patrick Ertel
Box 500
Missouri City, TX 77459

Engineers and Engines
Don Knowles
2240 Oak Leaf Street
P.O. Box 2757
Joliet, IL 60434–2757

Polk's Magazine
Dennis Polk
72435 SR 15
New Paris, IN 46553

Steam and Gas Show Directory
Iron Man Album
Gas Engine
Linda Weidman
41 North Charlotte Street
P.O. Box 328
Lancaster, PA 17608–0328

Index

**Moline Universal
advertisement**

Happy farmer and Case 10/18
Obviously pleased with his three-wheeled Case 10/18, this happy farmer pauses in his plowing work. (Glenbow Archives)

Deere 8010

When it was introduced in 1959, Deere's 8010 foreshadowed the future of farm tractors in its futuristic, articulated, four-wheel-drive design. Power came from a 215-hp, six-cylinder GM 6-71 engine and a nine-speed transmission. Unfortunately, only one hundred 8010's were built during 1960–1961, many of which were rebuilt as the subsequent 8020. Still, the future was cast, and there was no looking back. Owners: Walter and Bruce Keller. (Photograph by Chester Peterson Jr.)